WHY ME?
Seeking Answers in Your Grief

Surviving the Loss
of Your Child

Deborah Danielson
CFP®, CFS®, MSFS

"Seeing them in the STARS and appreciating them in every sunset."

DEDICATION

In loving memory of my son Jason who gave me every reason to tear my hair out but also to love him completely. You inspired me with your creativity and showed me this through all your talents. Although I never got to see you married or enjoy your potential children, God must have had a plan for your 24 years on earth. My promise is to share my story to help other parents in their darkest hour of need as they are grasping for answers to, Why ME?

COPYRIGHT

Copyright ©2017, Deborah L. Danielson
Printed in the United States of America.
ISBN - 978-0-9991949-0-4 (paperback)
Title: WHY ME? Seeking Answers in Your Grief: Surviving the Loss of Your Child

All rights reserved. The author retains ownership of all intellectual properties and copyrights to the book. No parts of this book can be reproduced, stored in a retrieval system, or transmitted by any means (written, electronic, digital, photocopy, audio or video recording, stored in a database or otherwise), nor used in a presentation without prior written permission of the copyright holder and author, except as permitted under Section 107 or 109 of the 1976 United States Copyright Act. The Author and Publisher specifically disclaim any liability, loss, or risk which is incurred as consequence, directly or indirectly, from the use and application of any of the contents of this work.

AUTHOR
Deborah L. Danielson
Deborah@DanielsonFinancial.com

PUBLISHER
Efluential Publishing
info@efluentialpublishing.com

Quantity discounts are available. To purchase, please **contact the author at**
Deborah@DanielsonFinancial.com
ISBN: 978-1-945578-08-3
Cover Price: $12.95

TABLE OF CONTENTS

ACKNOWLEDGEMENTS	7
INTRODUCTION	10
PART A: Your Challenges and Responsibilities	**12**
CHAPTER 1: Dealing With The Shock	13
CHAPTER 2: First Responses To Your Major Loss	17
CHAPTER 3: Making Arrangements	20
CHAPTER 4: It's Not About Denial; It's About Survival	25
PART B: Solutions to Your Challenges	**28**
CHAPTER 5: Getting Through The First Years	29
CHAPTER 6: Numbing My Mind	44
CHAPTER 7: Other Siblings	61
PART C: Issues and Ideas	**70**
CHAPTER 8: Questions You Will Ask Yourself, Questions Others Will Ask.	71
CHAPTER 9: Remembering Your Loved One	78
EPILOGUE: Feeling The Moment Of Death	83
APPENDIX: Support Organizations and Resources	88
About the Author	98

"Feeling secure in the knowledge they will never be FORGOTTEN and will always live on in YOUR HEART."

ACKNOWLEDGEMENTS

For those who helped me during the most trying and difficult week of my life I want you to know that your kindness, helpfulness, and just being there is so greatly appreciated more than words could ever express. You will never know how deeply you touched me and how much your kindness meant.

- Robert Allen, my soulmate, for emotional support and in helping me make the arrangements.
- Melissa Danielson, my daughter, for emotional support.
- Dwane Chance, my son-in-law, for emotional support.
- Marietta Brown, my mother, for emotional support.
- Charlotte Crist, my aunt, who flew out to help and stayed at the house
- Al Campbell, my brother-in-law, and Devin Campbell, my nephew, for helping with the song arrangements and performance at Jason's service.
- Bill Ruston and Gloria Roberts, dear friends, who picked up food, fixed everything and cleaned it up afterwards.
- Richard and Lyn Kaufman, dear friends, for brunch and playing potential music selections to help me decide what should be played at the service.
- Lyn Richman, a dear friend, who stayed at the house during the services.
- My Danielson Financial Group team who held down the office while I was away. You gave me peace of mind that I did not have to worry about my business. The greatest includes Stacy Simmer, Lindsay Wright, Carlene Gaydosh, Jay Pieper, Linda Becker, Sherri Myer, Kelly McAnally, Lyn Kaufman, Michael Carpenter, Jeanette Sanchez and Keith Lund.
- Larry Davis, funeral director, the most kind person, never rattled, who calmed us at Palm Mortuary while planning Jason's services.

And for those who helped with the creation of this book, thank you so much:

- Many thanks to Richard Faverty owner of Beckett Studios, photographer extraordinaire for the beautiful cover photo photograph. You always capture the perfect shot. www.beckettstudios.com
- Sydney LeBlanc, writer and editor, for polishing the content of the book.
- Cliff Pelloni, Efluential Publishing, for the amazing design/layout of the book and moving it over the finish line, allowing me to share it with the world.

INTRODUCTION

WHY?

I can't tell you how many times I've asked myself this question, but never getting an answer. My mind was worn raw thinking back and forth about why this happened to my son and why this happened to me. I know it sounds terribly self-centered, but I guess I never really thought how deeply this kind of death affects someone until it happened to me. The death of your child is an incredibly rude awakening to the real world. I felt like God had singled me out to take away one of my greatest treasures and I could not understand why. My son Jason was so young, only 24 years old, when he left this earth. I felt that his life was one yet to be lived and explored. He had just been accepted into the Le Cordon Bleu College of Culinary Arts. He seriously told me that next Thanksgiving— instead of me doing all the work for our extended large family— he was going to prepare the meal as our Chef. Life was just starting to really ramp up for him. He had a new girlfriend, was moving into a new apartment to be close to school, and had a new career path he was excited and passionate about. He felt like he finally made it when he was accepted into the Le Cordon Bleu.

WHY DID THIS HAPPEN?

As much as I want to know, I guess I'll never really know the answer to "why" this happened. All I can say at this point is it was a part of God's plan, certainly not mine. If I didn't believe this, I guess I would think there was some mean evil force out to destroy my life's happiness. I'm sure there are lessons I am to learn, but they are painful ones. I think it's maybe so I can be a better wife, mother, sister, friend and financial advisor. I have firsthand knowledge of how deeply disturbing and unsettling the death of a child can be and how it can rock the firmest of foundations. I hope my book will help those who feel this way, too.

WHY DID I WRITE THIS BOOK?

I don't know exactly what I was looking for, but I wanted answers, comfort and understanding when I went through my loss. Nothing had prepared me for this day, this forever, "life-changing moment." I was hungry for answers and information. The more I read, the more questions I had. I was still hungry for more. As a Certified Financial Planner™ I wanted to help my clients as they experienced their loss. I wanted to share my knowledge to help ease their pain in a non-clinical psychological way. I felt I had to be a provider, a resource for them to solve issues and help them through their transition. I also wanted to help other friends and to suggest to clients that they pass my book on to their own friends as well.

PART A:
YOUR CHALLENGES AND RESPONSIBILITIES

1 DEALING WITH THE SHOCK

WHY ME? Seeking Answers in Your Grief

NOTHING WILL EVER PREPARE YOU FOR THE SHOCK OF HEARING THAT YOUR CHILD HAS DIED.

I remember the very instant clearly because I was in the office and we were installing a new software system. It was extremely important that all of us were available for the two hours that the technical people were going to conference in and teach us what we needed to know. We never do this, but this time we put our phones on message so that everyone would not be disturbed during the class although we were in the office.

My husband, Robert, called several times in the afternoon only to get the message phone and he thought it was odd. So, Robert came to the office and in to our conference room and said he needed to speak to me. Not knowing the situation, I told him I was in an important meeting. He was quite insistent and said, "I really need to speak to you right now," so I excused myself and went just outside the hallway. I knew something was really wrong when he tried to talk to me and couldn't look me in the eye and seemed very upset.

Dealing with the Shock

HE STARTED BY SAYING, "I JUST DON'T KNOW HOW TO TELL YOU THIS."

He's never been a man of few words and can easily speak to anyone, and he looked down at his shoes and started to cry. I became deeply concerned, so I asked him, "Is it your mother? Your father? My mother? My father? What is it?" He then quickly blurted out the words, "Jason is dead." The pure shock and finality of those words dropped me to my knees. I knew it wasn't a joke, but I couldn't even begin to believe it was true. My mind was in a blur; I didn't know what to do or say.

He had been told by the coroner's office who came to our home carrying Jason's driver's license and asking, "Do you know him?" He explained to Robert that Jason had been in a car accident the night prior and was instantly killed. I remember going back to the conference room and my staff — who had heard my scream — knew something was really wrong. I let them know that Jason had died and I was going to go home and figure out what to do next. I was in total shock!

I have no way of knowing whether

it's better to know about impending or anticipated death due to someone's illness or whether to experience a sudden death that comes from nowhere. I know I felt robbed and cheated of a moment to say goodbye and that hurt me terribly. I felt it was cruel and unfair to not be able to talk to him one last time. The next time I saw his face was to view his body at the mortuary.

Although I knew it was him, it was not the young man so full of life and love that I remembered. Either way you lose a child is horrific. I think it is normal, but again I went back and thought to myself that this was very unfair and it was all about me.

> **THE DEATH OF A CHILD SHATTERS YOU; THERE'S NO WAY AROUND IT. YOUR ONLY SOLACE NOW IS TO LEARN TO DEAL AND LIVE WITH IT.**

2 FIRST RESPONSES TO YOUR MAJOR LOSS

CALLING FRIENDS AND FAMILY:

Right after this happened not only did I not have the ability to think straight, I promise if it happens to you, your mind will not stop for an instant day or night. Part of the responsibility is that you or someone in your family needs to make calls to friends and family members to let them know of the tragedy. This is extremely difficult, and for me it was done in a fog.

At that point I didn't know much about the car accident he had been in, just that it happened, although somewhere in the back of my mind I thought maybe it was a mistake and this was not real.....

But, if you call people and let them know what happened, usually their first question is, "How are you doing, are you okay?" And then they will ask, "Are you going to have a service?" They want to know so they can make their plans. Remember, if you have a lot of family out of town, you probably want to schedule something that gives them a little bit of time, at least a week, to make plane reservations and other things, just to be courteous.

Other than the immediate family, I didn't call a lot of people until I had gone down to the mortuary the next day and said, "What do we do? Lay this out for me. What decisions do I need to make?" That way you can call your friends and let them know the day and time of the service.

3 MAKING ARRANGE-MENTS

Making arrangements

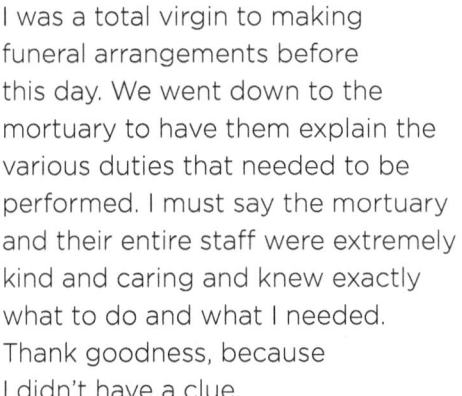

I was a total virgin to making funeral arrangements before this day. We went down to the mortuary to have them explain the various duties that needed to be performed. I must say the mortuary and their entire staff were extremely kind and caring and knew exactly what to do and what I needed. Thank goodness, because I didn't have a clue.

The next thing you know you're

LAUNCHED INTO AN EMOTIONAL AND FINANCIAL ENTANGLEMENT

of cremation, caskets, vaults, property, flowers, poems, music, speakers, food, obituaries, memorial videos, photos displays, remembrance cards and books and other displays. Decisions need to be made also regarding keeping ashes, scattering ashes, urns and who will get ashes.

When you have a big event and you want everything to be beautiful and perfect like a party or wedding you spend months to years planning it. When something like this happens the timeframe is so compressed that in a matter of hours to days decisions are made that are completely final.

YOU NEED TO HAVE SOMEBODY WITH YOU TO HELP YOU MAKE DECISIONS

because they just keep coming fast and furious and sometimes they feel beyond comprehension.

I worked on a memorial video encompassing Jason's life that normally would have taken months for me to prepare. I absolutely could not sleep for three complete 24-hour days nor did I feel tired.

Making arrangements

IT'S AMAZING WHAT YOU CAN DO WHEN YOU HAVE TO BECAUSE THERE IS NO OTHER CHOICE.

I was on a mission to get everything planned and completed. I worked tirelessly on putting together the photos and music for the video which I'm very proud of to this day.

I also spent lots of time going through photo albums — which was difficult and helpful at the same time — but going through photo albums is best when they are not on your iPhone. I couldn't remember how many pictures I needed to gather; maybe it was 50. So I just started with pictures of Jason when he was little, and pulled a couple here and a couple there. Before long, I had a pile of about 50 photos all the way up to age 24. That took time, and that was actually a good thing because it gave me something to do and that was a positive thing for me.

It's amazing what you can do when you have to because there is no other choice.

Somehow, we pull from that inner strength that we never knew we had and we almost take on a superhero status to work toward the completion
of all the things that need to be done.

BUT, IT'S IMPORTANT TO OCCUPY YOURSELF.

Some people might find some peace by visiting their church to meditate or pray.

4 IT'S NOT ABOUT DENIAL; IT'S ABOUT SURVIVAL

IT REALLY IS NOT ABOUT DENIAL IN THE FIRST FEW WEEKS OF YOUR LOSS.

I think it's about survival because you don't quite comprehend everything that has happened. Initially, you are surrounded by friends and family who come to offer condolences and help. Cards, flowers and books try to ease the transition, but after a few weeks they are all gone and the flowers have died. Suddenly, you come face-to-face with the reality of what has truly happened and you realize it was not a bad dream. You often wonder, "How can I pick myself up from this and go on as if nothing has happened?" While I don't think you can, there are ways to ease our own sorrow.

For me, one of the crazy things that seemed to happen in the first few months after Jason's death was I felt like I saw him in crowds or on the street.

It's not about denial; It's about survival

Think about this: When you first buy a new car it's interesting that all of a sudden you begin to see that car everywhere on the street, where prior to buying this new car you never noticed them. It's almost that same concept. I would look at a crowd of people walking by and from the back of one of the young men, I would swear he was Jason. My logical mind knew better, but somehow I had to walk quicker and get closer and just look to see and be sure it was not him.

Some days I felt I was really crazy. I remember one day seeing a group of young men and one who closely resembled him. I didn't, but I wanted to go up to him and say, "Can I just hug you?" I wanted so desperately to feel him just one more time.

PART B: SOLUTIONS TO YOUR CHALLENGES

5 GETTING THROUGH THE FIRST YEAR

IT DOESN'T GET BETTER — IT GETS DIFFERENT.

Eventually you learn to cope, but that does take a lot of time. Eventually, you can talk about it without crying. Time heals but, like a scar, it may fade but never goes away. You will never forget nor would you ever want to. The memories are the most precious things that you have and can hold onto when everything else is gone.

The first year was so difficult for me because no one had ever written a book about what to do. What is the protocol and what is the behavior?

Silly me; I wanted to act correctly, but I didn't know what that looked like. I had many questions like:

What do you do on his birthday?
- Do you celebrate it?
- Do you cry and mourn?
- Or do you pretend it didn't happen *(as if you would forget)*.

Getting through the first year

On Jason's first birthday I took the day off work, but really didn't tell anyone why. I just wasn't sure how I would react on that day, and if I could get through the day working with clients and be all right. The first anniversary of his death happened two weeks after his birthday and was scary for me. Once, again, I didn't know how I'd react so I booked a vacation to be gone.

That morning we got up and said a prayer for him and wished him well.

IT WAS GOOD TO BE GONE SO THAT WE DIDN'T HAVE TO FACE FAMILY OR FRIENDS THAT FIRST YEAR. I WASN'T SURE THAT I COULD.

Since then I realized that I did a disservice to his sister, Melissa, who was also suffering but I was too blind to realize at the time.

Now we get together as a family and we play that beautiful memorial video with pictures and music and celebrate his life from the beginning to the end. We talk about the good times and, of course, we still miss him but it gives us comfort even in our sadness.

I REALIZED WE NEEDED TO CREATE NEW TRADITIONS SO THINGS DIDN'T HURT SO MUCH.

Jason died on October 19th and his birthday was the 3rd which is quickly followed by his and my favorite season — the fall and Thanksgiving, and then Christmas. It made the first year of the holidays very challenging.

When my daughter Melissa got married several years later, a way that we remembered him as our family member is we put a beautiful framed picture of him on the chair with all the other wedding guests in attendance. So, in memory he attended as well and was remembered.

Friends of mine asked me, "What do you do with all the photos you have of him?" This is an extremely personal thing, but I was not going to take them down. He will always be my son and a part of the family and putting his pictures away will not make him disappear and, in fact, for me it would make me sadder. I realized that others in the family were concerned that maybe seeing his pictures would cause me to

DWELL ON HIM MORE AND SLOW DOWN MY GRIEVING PROCESS.

As I mentioned, everyone has separate and individual feelings and no one is right or wrong, but having his photos there gives me comfort and if someone would have taken them all down it would have been an even bigger shock to my system.

> **I'VE OFTEN BEEN ASKED, "WHAT YOU DO WITH ALL OF THE PERSONAL POSSESSIONS, OR HOW DO YOU CLEAN OUT HIS ROOM?"**

It was a bit easier for me because Jason had already moved out of our home. We went to his apartment a couple of days later to get clothes for his funeral to bring to the mortuary. At that time I took just a couple of things and photos that were sitting out on the dressers. As crazy as it seems, someone obviously knew he had died and broke into his apartment and stole just about everything there including the sheets off his bed and pillowcases.

Every single piece of clothing, ski outfits, skis, boots and jewelry were taken. So, there was nothing left for me to go through. This was also a big shock that hurt me, but there was nothing I could do. I gathered up a few videotapes, journals and books of his artwork to take with me. Even though it sounds bizarre, these items were worth more to me than the TV and stereo systems that were stolen.

A week after his death, I went to the towing yard where his truck had been impounded. Most of my friends thought this was crazy that I would want to see the vehicle he died in. I knew it was a horrific accident and every bone in his body was broken.

They had to cut him out of the car. The accident was his fault as he had crossed a car in passing in the other lane and was hit by a double semi tractor-trailer.

I took pictures that I still look at on rare occasions of that truck which is completely unrecognizable as a vehicle —even the tires were ripped off. It was amazing that there was anything at all left of him. Even though every bone in his body was broken and crushed,

GOD SPARED ME HIS FACE WHICH LOOKED BEAUTIFUL THE DAY OF HIS SERVICE

although the mortuary informed me that every other limb had been extremely maimed. Somehow, it was closure for me to want to see everything I could about the situation.

In the truck was a ski jacket he had just received for Christmas and one of his favorite shirts. I still have that shirt in a drawer that I may make a pillow or a throw out of someday. Right now I have not been motivated to do anything with them, except store them, and that's okay with me. Of course, I could have donated some of his clothes but when I approached one of his good friends, I said, "You know, this was Jason's jacket." And before I could finish, he said, "I would love to have it." I didn't know if he would love it or be creeped out. I was so happy that he wanted it. I also have Jason's artwork and I will frame some of it and also make a book of his art.

IF YOU HAVE ITEMS LIKE THIS, YOU MAY WANT TO SHARE THEM WITH THEIR FRIENDS AS THEY, TOO, ARE GRIEVING THE LOSS.

Getting through the first year

A friend of mine who lost her daughter, took her flannel shirt and sewed a pocket on it to fit a cell phone or another gadget. She embroidered her daughter's name on it and it was lovely. But just be careful of that first year. Don't go through all of your child's belongings and get rid of them. You may think that the memory of your child's things might be too painful. But you may regret it and feel like you have nothing left of your child because you gave everything away. Instead, you could just box things up and store them away. If you change your mind at some point, you can always donate them.

**IT HAD BEEN 12 YEARS SINCE JASON'S DEATH AND ALTHOUGH STILL NUMB I THOUGHT I WAS DOING PRETTY WELL.
YOU NEVER KNOW HOW SOMETHING CAN PULL YOU INTO THE ABYSS IN A HEARTBEAT.**

I was at home and had just picked up the mail and I saw this beautiful extra-large glossy post-card. When I read it, it said, "Congratulations to your new Cordon Bleu graduate." It had a picture of a young man in a chef coat and hat with the name Chef Jason embroidered on the jacket. I know it was exciting for all the other parents to see a postcard like this. We had certainly contacted the Cordon Bleu of his death just prior to starting the program and they were gracious enough to refund his tuition which I thought was only fair. Obviously, they did not remove our name from the mailing list of graduates two years later.

I can't tell you how long I looked at that postcard for days and weeks feeling somehow closer to him knowing what his destiny could have been.

THE PAIN OF RECEIVING THAT CARD WAS LIKE STABBING A KNIFE THROUGH MY HEART AND TEARING IT OUT ALL OVER AGAIN.

I thought I died another death that night. So you never know when something can pull you back to the bottom just when you're feeling like things are going to be okay.

Getting through the first year

> **I LEARNED THAT I NEED TO GIVE MYSELF PERMISSION TO FEEL THOSE MOMENTS BECAUSE THEY'RE CERTAINLY REAL AND TO DENY THEM WOULD BE TO PRETEND YOU'RE NOT HUMAN.**

I changed Jason's mailing address to mine so I could manage bills and notify credit card companies, etc. as they came in. It seems bizarre but I still get junk mail and solicitations for him 12 years later. No, it doesn't hurt now, but it's just surprising when they come in, and you'll need to brace yourself for this. I guess things happen in their own due course of time.

For example, I really wanted to write this book for 12 years. Sometimes I think if I really wanted to write it, I would have, but I just couldn't put myself through the pain. I now have crossed over to a point where it's easier to talk about, and more than anything I want to share my experience to ease the pain of someone going through it for the first time. If there's any tip or suggestion that can make their life easier I want to be that resource to them.

> I realize now how important it is to create new memories, new traditions and to change up the holidays so that they are truly celebrated for all those living, while not forgetting those who have gone before us.

Katherine's Story
PERSONAL REACTIONS THAT FIRST YEAR

During an interview with Robert T. Muller, Ph.D., a professor of psychology at York University, and the author of the book, "Trauma and the Avoidant Client", a woman who identified herself as Katherine described her personal reactions throughout the first year after the loss of her son, Ben, who was killed in a car accident 10 days shy of his 21st birthday. Said Katherine, "I decided to see a social worker a few months after Ben died. During the first few months after the accident, the only way I can describe how I was feeling is that there was no 'feeling.' It was as if my heart was ripped out and stomped on. There was nothing left, but a complete numbness."

Clinical psychologists Jennifer Buckle and Stephen Fleming, co-authors of Parenting after the Death of a Child: A Practitioner's Guide, commented that "this feeling of numbness described by Katherine, is often the first grieving experience reported by bereaved parents. Coupled with this sense of numbness, bereaved parents, especially mothers, feel vulnerable and unprotected in what is now considered to be an unfair world."

They continued, "Eventually the numbness subsides and the unsettling and preoccupying images of the child's death take over.

ALMOST ALL BEREAVED PARENTS MAKE REFERENCE TO TRAUMATIC MEMORIES.

Even parents not present when their child died describe the trauma experienced as if they were physically there and directly involved."

Grieving parents also fight with recurring flashes of past memories they shared with their deceased child. After a child's death, most parents feel as if a part of their life has been erased, this is a very frightening feeling. To cope, some parents will resort to avoiding places they associate with the deceased child.

BEREAVED PARENTS PUT A LOT OF ENERGY INTO AVOIDING FEELINGS, MEMORIES AND PLACES THAT REMIND THEM OF THE CHILD.

At times they also ruminate, thinking about what could or should have been.

So why do some parents have an easier time adjusting after the loss of a child, compared to others?

To move forward, grief counsellors tend to agree that parents need to experience their own pain, keep the deceased child's memory alive, and accept the loss. Parents who continue to avoid don't adjust so well. The ability to learn from bereavement helps parents take responsibility for creating a new purposeful life. Irvin Yalom, author of Existential Psychotherapy posits that when parents find it too painful to learn from their bereavement experience, they are unwilling to "feel true feelings guiltlessly."

FOR PARENTS TO ADJUST WELL, REALIZING THAT IT'S OKAY TO BE HAPPY AGAIN IS CRUCIAL.

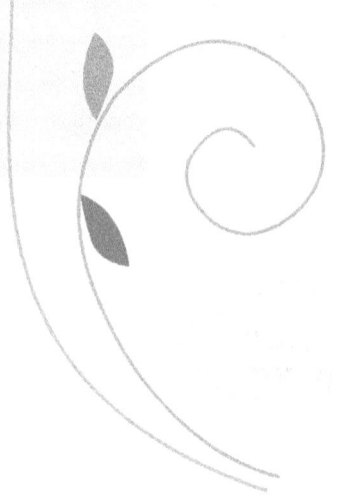

6 NUMBING MY MIND

WHAT DO YOU NEED TO DO TO NUMB YOUR MIND SO IT WILL STOP CONTINUALLY RELIVING THE PAST?

Especially in the early days and months, and the first year all of us find solace in different areas. For me, it was working to distraction.

I kept myself so booked with appointments and so busy in my social life that there would be no time for other thoughts to leak in. Maybe this wasn't healthy but it's just what I needed to do. The worst times of the day for me were in the shower when I was truly alone with my thoughts or in the evening when I went home from work. Thankfully, my commute home is very short. As soon as I got in to the car and turned it on, all these memories and thoughts came flooding back into my mind and often, before I left the parking lot, the tears were flowing so hard I couldn't see to drive. Often I would just sit there and cry and that was okay. I learned to dread driving alone as it made me think, grieve and hurt.

For others who are not workaholics like me, some may turn to drinking or drugs. And I am certainly not a health fanatic but I don't think either of these will do a body good. I would just caution you to take a close look and monitor your situation and don't let yourself slip down a slippery slope that's too difficult to get back up from.

But, I decided that to help numb my mind, I was going to go on a trip and so we took a family vacation and went to Cape Cod. My daughter said we needed to be on track this year. So, we had created a 10-minute memorial video that we showed at the service, and each year, on that day, we get together as a family and we watch the video. It starts when the kids were babies and it goes up to the present time. It has music, too. It's somber, but fun. It's a beautiful memory and we say a prayer before watching it to let Jason know we are thinking about him.

Here are a few comments from my daughter, Melissa Danielson, MEd, MS, LMFT, and she is a Licensed Marriage and Family Therapist with a Masters of Counseling in the state of Nevada in private practice[1]:

"I was in such a fog of pain and hurt from losing Jason that I started seeing a therapist to help me deal with my grief and sort out my pain. I saw Ann Allen, a psychologist at UNLV, for many months. I also went to group counseling, but didn't find that helpful, so I continued only individual therapy. I would also carry on conversations as if Jason was listening while driving on my way to places.

"Many times I would cry on my way to places in the car because it felt like the only time I could let it go. Driving with Jason was my way of keeping him alive with me since it felt like it was too uncomfortable for our family to talk about him. I think it is best to still talk about my brother and mention him in conversation with others. Hiding the fact that he existed feels much worse than trying to avoid being uncomfortable."

---

[1] http://danielsontherapy.com/

Melissa and I also attended an all-day program during the holidays. It was at a local church with a large facility. It included counseling by professionals about how to work through your grief, especially during the holidays and how to start new traditions, but realizing it's going to be different. Then, at the end of the day, we all went outside and got a balloon and a prayer was said; we then thought about our loved one(s) and then we released the balloon and it floated up and away. It was very special.

After a while, family and friends have heard enough and are just being kind when they're listening, but only hope you'll eventually shut up about it. About six months later at the support group meeting, I had an aha-moment that made me feel really good. I realized when a new family came in completely raw and miserable talking about their child's death that I was actually looking back on it with perspective.

I remember how it felt to be in that emotional state and actually felt like I had moved down the road and had actually made some healing strides because I wasn't in quite the same super miserable spot. Eventually, I stopped going too because I felt like I had made all the progress I could. I highly encourage those of you considering this option to do so because you will never find a more sympathetic and understanding group who are happy to listen because it helps all of you to heal.

A while after that, I remember reading an article by Paula Stephens, M.A.[7] who hosted the first worldwide online summit for grief recovery – "The Healthy Grief Revolution: A Survivor's Summit." She also offers the 28-Day Grief Detox to kick start your health after loss.

Dr. Stephens' article, "What I Wish More People Understood About Losing A Child" discussed the loss of her own child, Brandon, and her experiences at a local chapter of The Compassionate Friends, an organization solely dedicated to providing support for those who have lost children, grandchildren or siblings.

Said Dr. Stephens in her article, "Four and a half years after the death of my oldest son, I finally went to a grief support group for parents who have lost children. I actually went to support a friend who recently lost her son. I'm not sure I would've gone except that when I was in her shoes, four years ago, I wish I would've had a friend to go with me. Losing a child is the loneliest, most desolate journey a person can take and

THE ONLY PEOPLE WHO CAN COME CLOSE TO APPRECIATING IT ARE THOSE WHO SHARE THE EXPERIENCE."

---

[2] www.crazygoodgrief.com

WHY ME? Seeking Answers in Your Grief

She continued, "The support that I received while attending the sessions was remarkable and I learned several critical tips that not only helped me, but also helped friends of mine.

Here are the five tips that can be your own compass and also help you navigate how to give support to other grieving parents on a sacred journey they never wanted to take."

FIVE TIPS[3] FROM PAULA STEPHENS, MA

1. REMEMBER OUR CHILDREN

The loss of children is a pain all bereaved parents share, and it is a degree of suffering that is impossible to grasp without experiencing it first-hand. Often, when we know someone else is experiencing grief, our discomfort keeps us from approaching it head-on. But we want the world to remember our child or children, no matter how young or old our child was. If you see something that reminds you

---

[3] www.crazygoodgrief.com
www.mindbodygreen.com/0-17928/what-i-wish-more-peopleunderstood- about-losing-a-child.html

of my child, tell me. If you are reminded during the holidays or on his birthday that I am missing my son, please tell me you remember him. And when I speak his name or re-live memories re-live them with me, don't shrink away. If you never met my son, don't be afraid to ask about him. One of my greatest joys is talking about Brandon.

2. ACCEPT THAT YOU CAN'T "FIX" US

An out-of-order death such as child loss breaks a person (especially a parent) in a way that is not fixable or solvable — ever! We will learn to pick up the pieces and move forward, but our lives will never be the same. Every grieving parent must find a way to continue to live with loss, and it's a solitary journey. We appreciate your support and hope you can be patient with us as we find our way. Please: don't tell us it's time to get back to life, that's it's been long enough, or that time heals all wounds.

WHY ME? Seeking Answers in Your Grief

We welcome your support and love, and we know sometimes it is hard to watch, but our sense of brokenness isn't going to go away. It is something to observe, recognize, and accept.

3. KNOW THAT THERE ARE AT LEAST TWO DAYS A YEAR WE NEED A TIME-OUT

We still count birthdays and fantasize what our child would be like if he/she were still living. Birthdays are especially hard for us. Our hearts ache to celebrate our child's arrival into this world, but we are left becoming intensely aware of the hole in our hearts instead. Some parents create rituals or have parties while others prefer solitude. Either way, we are likely going to need time to process the marking of another year without our child.

Then there's the anniversary of the date our child became an angel. This is a remarkable process similar to a parent of a newborn, first counting the days, then months, then the one year anniversary, marking the time on the other side of that crevasse in our lives. No matter how many years go by, the anniversary date of when our child died brings back deeply emotional memories and painful feelings (particularly if there is trauma associated with the child's death). The days leading up to that day can feel like impending doom or like it's hard to breathe. We may or may not share with you what's happening.

This is where the process of remembrance will help. If you have heard me speak of my child or supported me in remembering him/her, you will be able to put the pieces together and know when these tough days are approaching.

WHY ME? Seeking Answers in Your Grief

4.
REALIZE THAT WE STRUGGLE EVERY DAY WITH HAPPINESS

It's an ongoing battle to balance the pain and guilt of outliving your child with the desire to live in a way that honors them and their time on this earth.

I remember going on a family cruise 18 months after Brandon died. On the first day, I stood at the back of the ship and bawled that I wasn't sharing this experience with him. Then I had to steady myself, and recognize that I was also creating memories with my surviving sons, and enjoying the time with them in the present moment.

As bereaved parents, we are constantly balancing holding grief in one hand and a happy life after loss in the other. You might observe this when you are with us at a wedding, graduation or other milestone celebration. Don't walk away — witness it with us and be part of our process.

5. ACCEPT THE FACT THAT OUR LOSS MIGHT MAKE YOU UNCOMFORTABLE

Our loss is unnatural, out-of-order; it challenges your sense of safety. You may not know what to say or do, and you're afraid you might make us lose it. We've learned all of this as part of what we're learning about grief.

We will never forget our child. And in fact, our loss is always right under the surface of other emotions, even happiness. We would rather lose it because you spoke his/her name and remembered our child, than try and shield ourselves from the pain and live in denial.

Grief is the pendulum swing of love. The stronger and deeper the love, the more grief will be created on the other side. Consider it a sacred opportunity to stand shoulder-to-shoulder with someone who has endured one of life's most frightening events. Rise up with us.

WHY ME? Seeking Answers in Your Grief

FEELING GUILTY?

In our situation, neither of us was responsible for the death of Jason so there never was a conflict. Many of these families we heard about in counseling felt responsible for the death of their child because they may have been the driver of the car, for example, or the one watching the child that fell into the pool, or did not keep a watchful eye on the person who drank the poison or those who felt they didn't have a harmonious home life and their child committed suicide. It is easier to blame someone else. I highly encourage couples counseling if there's any inkling of doubt. Guilt can be all consuming and detrimental not only to the family but also to the marriage.

Statistics show that about 20% of couples divorce after losing an infant all the way up to a 34-year-old child.

Numbing My Mind

NO TWO PEOPLE GRIEVE THE SAME... GIVE EACH OTHER THE SPACE TO GRIEVE DIFFERENTLY AND KNOW THAT IT IS OKAY.

No two people grieve the same; while some people can be very vocal, others turn everything inside. Losing a child is probably the hardest thing a couple could ever go through. Give each other space to grieve differently and know that it is okay. Crying too much or crying too little isn't a sign that you either do or you don't care. It's extremely important to continue to talk to family members and your spouse. We all move on within our own timetable.

Sometimes it's ironic when family stops talking about the death at all. One day I remember my brother was over visiting during the holidays and it was as if no one ever thought about Jason. I asked him why he never mentioned Jason ever again after the funeral. He said. "I didn't want to bring him up because I didn't want to cause you to cry." I let him know that it was safe and it was definitely okay to speak his name and talk about him.

By never mentioning him, it was as if he disappeared off the face of the earth and no one remembered and it felt even more hurtful to me than remembering. Eventually, talking about it and sharing memories can be cathartic and very helpful in the healing process and bring you great joy instead of pain.

MANY PEOPLE HAVE THEIR OWN WAYS OF DEALING WITH THEIR TRAGEDY.

Another good friend of mine lost her daughter in a car accident when she was 16. It has been about 18 years ago now and she continues to grieve constantly. I know she hasn't dealt with it and still leaves her daughter's room as a shrine. She still signs every birthday card, Christmas card, and everything with her name on it, too. But if it makes her feel better, she may be able to deal with it sooner.

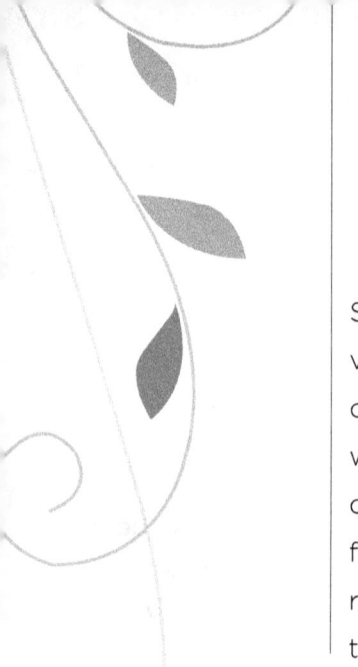

Some people might want to do some volunteering during this time — for the church, for other social organizations who really need volunteers to help others in need. If you do, it makes you feel good, it's meaningful and you realize there are others who are in pain, too.

6 OTHER SIBLINGS

If I felt any guilt a few years later for the things that I did not do or could have done better this is an area in which I plead guilty.

I WAS SO CONSUMED WITH MY OWN GRIEF THAT I COULDN'T SEE PAST MY OWN NOSE.

It was as though I had forgotten that my daughters also experienced the same loss that I had. I forgot how deeply they were grieving too, and I needed to be there for them as well. Sometimes they were mad, sad, or even feeling guilty.

P. Gill White, Ph.D. author, *Sibling Grief: Healing after the Death of a Sister or Brother* provides numerous answers to why bereaved siblings are still mad — days, months, or even years after the death of their brother or sister.

Other Siblings

Below are some of the reasons[1] that Dr. White explains — I think they will help you understand more about the type of grief they are feeling and how you can help them:

1. Others expected the surviving sibling to take care of the parents or to make up for the loss.

2. How they were treated immediately after hearing the news. Some were ignored, some were sent to stay with a relative, some were not given any information.

3. Because of the way that they, or another sibling, was treated in the months and years after the loss. For example, some were blamed for not being the one who died, some were targeted as a scapegoat for the parent's anger.

---

[1] Dr. White's website, "The Sibling Connection"
www.counselingstlouis.net/page13.htm

4. Their peers had no awareness of the reality of life and death, so they felt as if they were now different from them.

5. Because life went on as normal.

6. They were not allowed to grieve or were encouraged to feel guilty for grieving.

7. No one talked about the death and the dead sibling was never mentioned.

8. They didn't get to see the body.

9. They don't agree with some aspect of the funeral burial site, or gravestone.

10. They don't feel the sibling got the appropriate care while in the hospital.

11. They saw the body in a broken and wounded state, after a car accident, for example.

12. They were not allowed or encouraged to go to, or participate in, the funeral.

13. They didn't know how to deal with their feelings.

14. They weren't informed about the severity of their sibling's illness.

Other Siblings

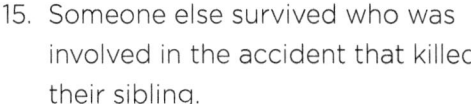

15. Someone else survived who was involved in the accident that killed their sibling.

16. They had to babysit, clean house, or be responsible for other chores while parents were at the hospital, sheriff's office, funeral home, etc.

17. No one ever asked how they were feeling. They often heard "How are your parents?"

18. They had to grow up overnight.

19. They were blamed for acting out and trying to get attention, when they were too young to understand what was really happening.

20. They were over-protected after the loss.

21. They were expected to "become" the dead sibling.

22. They didn't get a chance to say good-bye.

23. The dead sibling's belongings were given away or

24. Disposed of without their consent.

All I can say is take a moment and consider that their needs are just as real as yours, if not more so. Yes, they experience it in a different way, but the pain is just as real for them. Try to support them in any way you can and involve them so they don't feel like they're on their own dealing with their own issues. This is a family in healing, not just individuals in healing. We all need to experience new traditions to continue enjoying the best of each other without forgetting the loved one who is not there with us.

I MUST TELL YOU ONCE I GOT THROUGH SOME OF MY INITIAL HEALING, I STARTED GETTING CONCERNED ABOUT A NEW PARANOIA OF MINE: FEAR OF LOSS AGAIN.

It's hard not to become overprotective and afraid of losing again. Every time my daughters went somewhere, the thought crossed my mind, "what if they did not come back again?" The idea of them texting or taking phone calls while driving made me crazy.

THE THOUGHT OF GOING THROUGH THIS ANOTHER TIME WAS UNIMAGINABLE.

When they tell you they're leaving to travel to areas of the country that you think may be unsafe, it's hard to keep your mouth shut and not become a mom and tell him/her to stay home.

I had to remember that they do have a life of their own and they do make their own decisions. My newfound paranoia has nothing to do with reality; it only has to do with my fear of loss again. I must say I don't think there's enough strength in the world that I could muster to go through this another time.

Melissa had a few things to say about sibling grief (her own):

"As much as losing my brother, Jason, gave me a permanent void, it did bring my mother and me closer. I realized I was only idealizing Jason to help me grieve him, even though he had a few bad traits. She became a better mom after he passed away. As much as I didn't want him to leave, it did give her more room to give me attention.

"That's the truth, but that being said, in my studies to be a counselor, one of the main premises we are taught is to cause no harm. I went to see a huge international speaker for a breakthrough seminar. I ended up sharing my story of losing my brother. The speaker decided to make me his "learning example."

He said that by Jason dying I got what I wanted: a relationship with my mom. He was cruel and did cause harm. It hurt me deeply that he accused me of wanting my brother dead.

I told my parents about my traumatic experience in his seminar and they rallied around me. My stepdad went off about what a terrible person the speaker was, and that his hypothesis was sick and disturbing. I only bring this up because I went to lots of self-help seminars to help heal the void of my loss. I warn others to research who you decide to be vulnerable to. The fact that my mom and stepdad defended me immediately, and were so furious that this PhD had used me in class, made healing faster because I felt loved and supported."

PART C: ISSUES AND IDEAS

8 QUESTIONS YOU WILL ASK YOURSELF OTHERS WILL ASK YOU

WHY ME? Seeking Answers in Your Grief

FEELING GUILTY IS AN EMOTION THAT CAN OVERTAKE A PARENT

Guilt can be all-consuming and detrimental not only to the family but also to the marriage. Here are just a few of the questions you will ask yourself as well as those other people will ask you:

- Why didn't I see it coming?
- Why didn't I prevent it?
- Why didn't we find a better doctor sooner?
- Why wasn't I there?
- How can I ever forgive myself?

Your answers, of course, will depend on the circumstances surrounding the death of your child, i.e., automobile accident, drug addiction, a medical condition etc. For example, I have a friend whose child committed suicide and she kept asking herself, "Why didn't I see the signs that something was wrong?" "Why didn't I see that he/she was depressed?"

But you look back and wonder if you really saw any signs.

You just get busy with your own life..... and then when you step back and reflect on it, you realize that in your day to day life, you don't take the time to really think day to day about what might be going on "under the radar" when you are not paying attention. And now you're dwelling on it, where before it was just a day to day thing.

But the guilt element is rough. You might be saying to yourself, "How can I ever forgive myself?" Well, you always think you have tomorrow. Tomorrow is another day and this problem will solve itself. And when the person has passed, you realize, "I needed to have taken the time then to find another doctor, or a rehab institution" or whatever the problem may have been.

Could you have done more? Could you have done better? Should you have tried again? Could you have found a better cancer doctor, for example? Could I have tried harder? Could I have challenged the insurance company to do something? Maybe. So many questions you will ask yourself, and everyone does it... and sometimes it just makes you feel worse.

One Question That is Always Difficult to Answer

What do you say when you are asked, "How many children do you have?" Something I still struggle with is how to respond when someone asks me how many children I have. It just happened to me recently. I just said, "Two." It was easier than saying, "Well, I did have three, but my son died when he was 24 years old." And if I say that, and they don't know me that well, they will say, "Oh, I'm so sorry!" But I feel like if I say two, part of me feels like I'm being disingenuous—that I'm not honoring the memory of my son.

I STILL STRUGGLE WITH HOW TO RESPOND WHEN SOMEONE ASKS ME HOW MANY CHILDREN I HAVE.

And so it always makes me wonder, "What do I say?" I've heard other people who have lost a child say, "Well, I have two here on earth and one in heaven. And I think that sounds nice. But then you wonder, if somebody says that to you, do you say, "Oh, okay," as opposed to, "Oh, so, what happened to your child?" But you don't want them to leave thinking, "Okay, I wonder what happened. Maybe I shouldn't talk to that person anymore; maybe I hit the wrong cord," or something like that. For some people that's an easy answer, and for others, it's not. For me, I guess it comes down to "depends on if you want the short answer or the long answer."

Of course if it's a casual encounter like someone you just met at the grocery store and you are just chatting for a few minutes and they might say, "Oh, I have three children, how many do you have?"

WHY ME? Seeking Answers in Your Grief

This person could be a stranger or someone you don't know well, and my opinion is that they don't need to know anything else.

My friend who lost her daughter had a terrible experience a few years after her death. Someone asked, "Do you have children?" And she went, "Uh," and ran out of the kitchen crying. Everybody sat there and went, "What did we do?" Somebody came and found me and said, "I don't know what happened, but we just asked her this, and she went running out of the room like her hair was on fire." I said, "She lost her daughter a year or two ago, and certainly wasn't ready for it." She's still not.

Each parent who has experienced the death of a child has his or her own unique way of responding to the question of "how many children do you have?" Just remember, there's no "right" or "wrong" way to respond, nor is there anything wrong with answering the question in various ways at different times. Sometimes it will just depend on your mood and the circumstances. Bottom line: what's important is that you honor your feelings.

PSYCHICS

What?! Psychics? Yes, you read correctly. And what do psychics have to do with grief? In reality, not much, however I have heard about many instances where the parent who has lost a child is desperate and grieving so much they will do just about anything to have the chance to communicate with the spirit of their child.

My husband, who produced MindVention, the world's best mentalist convention did not believe in psychics and had his own beliefs in what psychics can and cannot do. He would talk about those who say, "I can talk to the dead and I can channel their spirits and communicate what they say to the person who is grieving." If you think they are a bit shady, you may be right.

My husband believed, as I do, that it may not be the best avenue to travel down... so reconsider hiring a psychic. If someone tries to convince you that a certain psychic they know can help you, just be very wary. Sometimes they may be trying to take advantage of your fragile state. Just stick with authentic sources of help like counseling groups, therapists, and community and church support.

9 REMEMBERING YOUR LOVED ONES

When my son died I had no idea how vital it would be for me to create tangible ways of remembering him. But I've found over time that it is incredibly important that he is thought of as a cherished member of our family and that people feel comfortable remembering him along with us.

THE ETHEREAL TIE IN LIFE AND BEYOND DEATH, "THE SILVER CORD"

Even though we may have lost a child, we still want to feel them near. It's comforting to believe that you can't sever the connection between you even if you wanted to. Some call this ongoing connection The Ethereal Tie that extends beyond death, "The Silver Cord."

Soon the time will come when you will want to honor your child, and in a way that will be memorable, permanent, and close to your heart.

Take some time to choose the way in which you will honor him or her and remember you can choose several ways to do so, it's all up to you. Here are a few ways other parents have honored their child that you may want to consider:

1. SCHOLARSHIPS

You might consider a scholarship to your local community college, and fund it in your child's name. It could be a one-time thing or it could be an endowment. Some parents may have already started a college fund for their child who was not attending college yet. For example, I had a client whose child passed away, and instead of doing a 529 plan which is a tax-advantaged savings plan, they did a pre-paid scholarship program here in Nevada. (Unfortunately, it is not refundable. In the earlier years of these programs they paid a certain amount and they guaranteed it would pay for college.)

So, the scholarship can be designated under your child's name as a memorial scholarship. Students will write an essay as to why they might be the most deserving to have four years of college paid.

2. DONATIONS TO CHILDREN'S ORGANIZATIONS AND CHARITIES/ FOUNDATIONS

- Make a Wish Foundation
- Big Brothers/Big Sisters
- Boys and Girls Clubs of America
- March of Dimes
- St. Jude Children's Research Hospital
- Shriner's Hospital for Children

3. MEMORIALS
- Benches
- Paving stones
- Home garden markers
- Plant a tree in their honor
- Adopt a section of the highway in their name

4. WRITE A BOOK ABOUT THEIR LIFE

5. PUBLISH BOOKS OF THEIR ART, MUSIC, POEMS OR PHOTOGRAPHY

6. NAME A STAR AFTER THEM
(International Star Registry)

www.starregistry.com

EPILOGUE

FEELING THE MOMENT OF DEATH

This may be the most unusual part of my story you read, but I swear every word of it is true. The night of Jason's death (which I would have no way of knowing until the next day), I was on my computer working in my home office. I've been working away for several hours and thought I had better finish up and start getting ready for bed.

Before I finished what I was working on, I had no idea what it was that came over me, but I felt it physically in every inch of my body. I thought of Jason and I felt the most overwhelming feeling of love for him radiating warmth physically going right through my entire body. It almost felt like standing in front of a fireplace with the flames lapping on my skin. I looked in the right-hand corner of my computer and saw the time was 9:30 PM.

Feeling the moment of Death

I picked up my phone and called Jason's cell phone, but he didn't answer. I left him a long voicemail letting him know that I was thinking about him, missing him and how very much I loved him and to give me a call back at his earliest convenience. It was just such a poignant feeling that I can't explain, but it was very, very real.

I didn't think anything about it until the next night. Later, when Robert and I spoke about the coroner coming to the home and he said the time of death was 9:30 PM, I was so amazed because I know that Jason was communicating with me and I felt him pass through me on his way out of this world.

Maybe it was his arms hugging me in a warm embrace for the last time and, of course, I just didn't recognize it for what it was then. I will never know how to explain what this was, only that I know it happened and it was very real and I physically felt it through every inch of my body. The police department knew who to call because they looked at his cell phone and saw the last message that came in was mine.

LAST WORDS

Thank you for reading my book. I wrote it initially for myself as a healing process. I also wrote it for you to help you go through your grief journey and to make it easier. I know it's taken me a long time to get to that point; more than 12 years. Don't forget: it's never too late to go back and remember your loved ones and do some of the things you never thought of doing. Even if you're reading this book long after the death of your child, you might say, "Well it's too late to attend a counseling group, or to do a memorial." It's never too late. I hope that the book has helped you as much as it's helped me while I was writing it for you. Much love and blessings on your journey.

SUPPORT ORGANIZATIONS AND RESOURCES
C.O.P.E. Foundation
(Connecting Our Paths Eternally)

A grief and healing organization dedicated to helping parents and families living with the loss of a child

COPEline: (516) 364-COPE (2673)
COPE PO Box 1251
Melville, NY 11747
Karen Flyer, Executive Director (516) 484-4993
www.copefoundation.org

Valley of Life
Established as an online memorial site where families and friends can memorialize their loved ones forever. Valley of Life has become a premiere resource for funeral planning, grief support and bereavement resources. The site offers an online funeral notice service, customized photo albums, and personalized online memorials for users.

http://www.ValleyofLife.com

American Association of Suicidology
Dedicated to the Understanding and Prevention of Suicide Since 1968, this nonprofit organization. has helped family and friends who have lost a loved one to suicide. Find survivor support groups, peer counseling, and other services.

Suite 310, 4201 Connecticut Avenue NW,
Washington, DC 20008
(202) 237-2280
http://www.suicidology.org/

The Candlelighters Childhood Cancer Foundation
Because Kid's can't fight cancer alone!

This group was founded more than a quarter of a century ago to provide advocacy, support, and information for families and survivors of childhood cancer. It is the largest and oldest pediatric cancer organization in the country.

7910 Woodmont Ave, Suite 460
Bethesda MD 20814
(301) 657-8401
www.candle.org

The Compassionate Friends, Inc.
The Compassionate Friends is a nationwide mutual self-help bereavement organization offering friendship, understanding, and hope to bereaved families that have experienced the death of a child at any age from any cause. TCF/USA has nearly 600 chapters with locations in all 50 United States plus Washington DC and Puerto Rico.

PO Box 1347
Oak Brook, IL 60521
(877) 969-0010 or (630) 990-0010
https://www.compassionatefriends.org/when-a-child-dies/

The Erika Whitmore Godwin Foundation and GriefHaven

Providing hope and support for parents and others after the loss of a child.

15332 Antioch Street, #147
Pacific Palisades, CA 90272-3628
(310) 459-1789
www.griefhaven.org

MADD Mothers Against Drunk Driving

Making a difference for more than 20 years

Fathers and mothers from all over the country join this well-known nonprofit organization to find solace when a child is killed by a drunk driver.

PO Box 541688
Dallas, TX 75354-1688
800.GET-MADD (800) 438.6233
www.MADD.org

Moyer Foundation

The Moyer Foundation was created in 2000 by former Major League Baseball pitcher Jamie Moyer and his wife Karen What started as a small nonprofit in Seattle, WA, with a broad mission to help children in distress, has grown into a national organization with signature programs reaching thousands of children impacted by grief or addiction in their family in over 50 cities each year.

One Penn Center
1617 JFK Blvd, Suite 935
Philadelphia, PA 19103
(267) 687-7724

Seattle Office
2426 32nd Ave W. Suite 200
Seattle, WA 98199
(206) 298-1217

www.moyerfoundation.org

National SIDS Resource Center (Sudden Infant Death)
This group offers a wide variety of publications and support for those who have suffered loss due to SIDS.

8201 Greensboro Drive, Suite 600
McLean, VA 22102
(703) 821-8955
www.cdc.gov/sids/index.htm

Parents of Murdered Children

For the families and friends of those who have died by violence

Following the murder of their daughter Lisa, Charlotte and Bob Hullinger launched this nonprofit group in 1978. Support groups are available around the country, as well as legal advice, a newsletter, grief support weekends, and other services.

100 East Eighth Street, Suite B-41
Cincinnati, Ohio 45202
(513) 721-5683

http://www.pomc.com/

Pregnancy and Infant Loss Center

Following the murder of their daughter Lisa, Charlotte and Bob Along with a parent-to-parent outreach program, PILC offers educational materials, a newsletter, and information on counseling services. PILC can also connect parents with national and international support groups.

1415 E. Wayzata Blvd.
Wayzata, MN 55391
(612) 473-9372

http://nationalshare.org/

Grief Helps

On this blog you'll find a large assortment of grief helps: ideas and suggestions, words and images, mini-books and mini-videos. All of these are designed solely with grieving people in mind. And every resource offered here is absolutely free.

www.griefhelps.com

In Loving Memory

An organization specifically for bereaved parents who are now childless. The purpose of In Loving Memory is to provide conferences for bereaved parents who are now childless, where they find encouragement and solace from the profound grief caused by the death of their child.

Fair Lakes Hyatt, Fairfax, VA
http://www.inlovingmemoryconference.org/

LAS VEGAS AND SURROUNDING AREAS SUPPORT GROUPS FOR GRIEF OR GRIEVING

Adams Place

Provides support in a safe place where children, teens, young adults, caregivers and their families grieving a death can share their experiences. Offers a leading library and activities. A place where hope, warm hearts, and friendly ears help heal. Program is run by donations and trained volunteers. Adam's place does not charge a fee for its services.

601 S Rancho Dr., Bldg. C #19
Las Vegas, NV 89107
Kelly Boyers-Office: (702) 333-2326
www.adamsplaceforgrieflasvegas.org

Survivors of Suicide Support Group

Support group meets twice a month for people who have lost a loved one to suicide. Call for time and location.

Canyon Ridge Christian Church
6200 W. Lone Mountain Rd
Las Vegas, NV 89130
Sharon Thoren - (702) 496-0177
Church Main Phone - (702) 658-2722

www.survivorsofsuicide.org

Survivors of Suicide Loss Support Group – Henderson

Support group meets twice a month for people who have lost a loved one to suicide. Call for time and location.

2651 Paseo Verde, Suite 180
Henderson, NV
Linda Flatt – (702) 807-8133

https://nvsuicideprevention.org/support-groups/

Divorced & Widowed Adjustment, Inc.

Provides a weekly support group for those dealing with the death of a loved one; such as a spouse, parent, child, or friend. Call for information on when the group is held. Meetings every week at:

First Christian Church
101 S. Rancho Drive, Room # 4
Las Vegas, Nevada 89106
Park Baker, President-(702) 735-5544 (Open 24/7)

http://www.info4nv.org/

Central Christian Church, Support Group

Provides a grief support group for adults. Grief is a natural, emotional response to loss, but it can feel overwhelming. You can't avoid it, but you can understand it. You can find comfort in the midst of your pain. Call for information on when this group is held.

1001 New Beginnings Drive,
Henderson, NV 89011
Jud Wilhite, Senior Pastor (702) 735-4004

https://www.centralonline.tv/

Center for Compassionate Care

Provides self-help support groups for children, teens, adults, and families who have suffered a death to help them cope with the loss. Call for meeting details.

4131 S. Swenson Street
Las Vegas, NV 89119
Susan Condron-(702) 796-3167

http://www.nah.org/center-for-compassionate-care

Families of Murder Victims Support Group

Support group for families of murder victims.

2375 E. Tropicana Ste. 213
Las Vegas, NV 89119
(702) 564-5919

Bereaved Parents of the USA- Nevada Chapter

Support for parents, grandparents, and children of siblings that have died from any cause, at any age, including miscarriage and stillbirth. Holds an annual candle and balloon launch ceremony in December. Publishes quarterly newspaper, has lending library.

3963 Goldspur Street
Las Vegas, NV 89129
(702) 655-5538

Support for the Loss of a Loved One- Henderson & Las Vegas Locations

Receive support for the loss of a loved one through the Bereavement Support Group which meets the 2nd and 4th Wednesday of each month and 6:00 pm. Call for information.

Barbara Greenspun Women's Care Center of Excellence
100 N. Green Valley Parkway Suite 330
Henderson, NV 89074-Hendersob

7220 S. Cimarron Road Suite 195
Las Vegas, NV 89113-Vegas
(702) 616-4900
Hotline: (702) 616-4901

ABOUT THE AUTHOR

Deborah L. Danielson, CFP®, CFS®, MSFS

Deborah L. Danielson is owner and President of Danielson Financial Group. As a Las Vegas native, she has been an investment professional since 1981. Ms. Danielson is a CERTIFIED FINANCIAL PLANNER™ professional and has a Master's of Science in Financial Services.

In addition to being the author of Why Me? Ms. Danielson is also a co-author of several books including, The Expert's Guide to Financial Planning and Big Vision, Small Business... The Four Keys to Finding Success and Satisfaction as a Lifestyle Entrepreneur. She also has been published in Money Magazine, The Wall Street Journal, Dow Jones Wire, Bloomberg, and has appeared on local and national news and radio shows. She served as the Financial Editor for Nevada Woman magazine July 1995 and its replacement magazine, LV Woman, until 2008. Ms. Danielson has been a guest on FOX Business, CNBC Squawk on the Street and Power Lunch and BNN. She has appeared on newscasts live from the floor of the NASDAQ and an opening bell ceremony on the floor of the New York Stock Exchange.

Ms. Danielson employs a comprehensive, client-focused approach to financial planning that encompasses each client's financial goals, time frames and risk tolerance. In recognition of her extraordinary efforts, Ms. Danielson was named one of the Top 1200 Financial Advisors nationwide by Barron's Magazine February 2014, 2015, 2016 & 2017. She was also honored as one

---

[1] Barron's Top 1200 Financial Advisors, Barron's Top 100 Women Financial Advisors and Barron's Top 1000 Financial Advisors are based on assets under management, revenue produced for the firm, regulatory record, quality of practice and philanthropic work.

of the Top 1000 Financial Advisors nationwide by Barron's Magazine February 2009, 2010, 2011, 2012, & 2013; named one of the Top 100 Women Financial Advisors by Barron's Magazine, June 2008, 2009, 2010, 2011, 2012, 2013, 2014 & 2016; and Deborah was also listed as one of the Top 200 Wealth Advisors by Forbes in 2016 & named by Forbes as one of the Top 200 Women Advisors in 2017.

Ms. Danielson is actively involved in the professional association, International Women's Forum (IWF), and has been acknowledged for her leadership contribution. She is a founding member of the National Association of Women Business Owners, Southern Nevada Chapter; the past President and former board member of the Las Vegas Chamber of Commerce; and the past President of the Financial Planning Association (FPA) Las Vegas Chapter.

---

[2] Registered Rep Magazine Award based on assets under management.

[3] Goldline Research Award based on client references, experience, advanced certifications and services offered among other factors.

[4] The 2016 & 2017 Forbes Top 200 Wealth Advisors is based on minimum of [7] years as an advisor, one year with current firm, must be recommended or nominated by firm, quantities data such as revenue, assets under management and qualitative data such as compliance records, credentials, service model as well as other factors.

She obtained her WSET (Wine & Spirit Education Trust) Advanced Certificate, level three in pursuit of the Masters of Wine designation. Ms. Danielson and her husband (deceased) have raised three children and are now the proud grandparents of four wonderful grandchildren. Ms. Danielson is an avid traveler — 88 countries and counting — and enjoys collecting wine for her 3000 bottle wine cellar.

www.ingramcontent.com/pod-product-compliance
Lightning Source LLC
Chambersburg PA
CBHW071725040426
42446CB00011B/2219